CHANAKYA

HIS TEACHINGS AND ADVICE

CHANAKYA

HIS TEACHINGS AND ADVICE

ASHWANI SHARMA

JAICO PUBLISHING HOUSE

Ahmedabad Bangalore Bhopal Bhubaneswar Chennai
Delhi Hyderabad Kolkata Lucknow Mumbai

Published by Jaico Publishing House
A-2 Jash Chambers, 7-A Sir Phirozshah Mehta Road
Fort, Mumbai - 400 001
jaicopub@jaicobooks.com
www.jaicobooks.com

CHANAKYA: HIS TEACHINGS AND ADVICE
ISBN 81-7224-602-1

First Jaico Impression: 1998
Twelfth Jaico Impression (Enlarged edition): 2010
Twenty-fourth Jaico Impression: 2017

Printed by
Sanman & Co.
7/C/48, Sonawala Building
Tardeo, Mumbai - 400 007
E-mail: rajukothari1954@gmail.com

Contents

On Woman

WHEN THE LORD* OF THE THREE WORLDS WAS unsuccessful in resisting the charms of woman, than how can one denounce an ordinary human being for being deluded by her? A woman is an enchanting, alluring and gratifying sight, and she wields more power than God in enticing mankind.

TO LIBERATE HIMSELF FROM THE CLUTCHES OF this mirthless world, Man must worship God with pure devotion. To attain the pleasures of celestial life, he must adhere strictly to ethical and scriptural instructions. If this is impossible, then he must atleast take care not to

---

* Lord Vishnu lifted Govardhan on his finger to save the people from a possible cataclysm that could have been caused by Indra, the Rain God.

be captivated by womanly graces. Those who do not do any of the above, dissipate precious energy, and dawdle away their youth.

IT IS ALWAYS ESSENTIAL TO SAVE MONEY, FOR adversity pounces on one most unexpectedly. A man can attract a woman, only if he has wealth. But he must never lose sight of the fact, that they are both fickle in nature. Both money and woman can deceive him at any moment.

A MAN MUST GIVE PARTICULARLY CAREFUL consideration to marriage, for any decision taken in haste can ruin his life forever. He must always marry into a family which enjoys an equal status in society. A girl may have no physical charms, but if she hails from a family with an illustrious lineage, then he must not hesitate to marry her, for beauty is merely skin deep. But even if a girl is a ravishing beauty, if she belongs to a unworthy family, he must not accept her as his wife.

A WOMAN IS BELIEVED TO BE MORE DELICATE than a man. But a woman is four times more brazen than a man. She also has six times his courage and eight times his strength of passion.

A MAN MUST SHOW GREAT REGARD FOR HIS queen, his mother-in-law, and the wives of his friend and his master. Those men who form, or approach women with the intention of forming illicit relationships with them, are the most morally depraved persons. In each religion women are treated with great respect. They are the adored ones.

THE THREAD OF LOVE IS EXTREMELY STRONG. Bhoinra had the capacity to cut through wood. But after entering the lotus he was unable to come out, even after attempting to pierce its petals. A powerful bond of love existed between the petals and the flower. The world has seen no stronger ties than those of love.

WHEN A MAN IS DECEIVED BY THE NOTION THAT a woman has fallen in love with him, he is unaware of the fact that he has become a mere puppet in her hands.

A FRIVOLOUS WOMAN WHO PRATTLES incessantly, pays a great deal of attention to the gestures of others, and constantly muses over other persons, cannot maintain her fidelity. She is bound to indulge in sexual affairs with other men.

A WOMAN WHO OBSERVES FASTS WITHOUT THE tacit consent of her husband reduces his longevity. She is condemned to eternal hell.

EVEN IF A WOMAN GIVES AWAY EVERYTHING that has been bestowed upon her, observes various fasts, lives a life of abstinence, and visits all the places of pilgrimage, she cannot become pure of heart. But she is definitely cleansed of all sins, if she worships at the feet of her husband.

THERE IS A CUSTOM PREVALENT IN NEPAL, according to which a married woman washes the feet of her husband with water from a copper vessel. Daily, she drinks the same water with which she washed her husbands feet. She believes that this act lengthens her husband's life, and makes him healthy, wealthy and happy.

DUPLICITY, ABRUPT DISPLAYS COURAGE, coquetry, deception, greed, profligacy and quarrelsomeness are the natural characteristics of a woman. One must not feel confounded, seeing her behave this way.

ONLY A CHASTE, ASTUTE, VIRTUOUS AND mellifluent woman, who remains faithful to her husband, truly deserves his patronage. Such a wife is a godsend to any man. Blessed, is the man, who has found such a woman to be his wife.

HOW CAN ONE REPROACH THE ORDINARY MAN, when even the Gods, and eminent persons with a profound knowledge of Sanskrit, avidly seek to taste the elixir of life on a woman's lips? A woman is a truly powerful obsession.

WHAT IS MAN'S GREATEST FASCINATION? IT IS the woman. She is the hub around which his mind revolves. A man is powerfully influenced by her captivating, coquettish ways. She soon succeeds in confining him to a prison of passion and irrational behaviour.

EVEN AN EXCEPTIONALLY BEWITCHING WOMAN with perfect, chiselled features, is a bag of flesh, blood and bones after all. Yet man, maddened and intoxicated by his youth and love, drowns himself in a maelstrom of endless pain and suffering.

TO ABSTAIN FROM A WOMAN'S ENCHANTING ways, is the greatest virtue.

"YOU OLD HAG! WHAT ARE YOU LOOKING FOR? Have you lost something?"

"OH STUPID MAN! I AM LOOKING FOR MY LOST youth." pat came the reply from the old hag.

EVEN AS A WOMAN GETS OLDER, SHE continues to cling to the illusory notion that she is younger than her age.

SHE ENDEAVOURS TO LOOK AS CAPTIVATING AS possible, in an effort to prolong her youth indefinitely.

WHY HAS A MAN MERELY TO BEHOLD A WOMAN'S graceful form and winsome charm, to have his passion ignited? Women are intrinsically similiar, and there is little variation, even in the sexual satisfaction that man derives from them.

OFTEN A MAN IS IMMEASURABLY AROUSED BY a woman's graceful form and bewitching allure. Since man is by nature polygamous, he craves for sexual relations with a variety of women. In this mad pursuit, he becomes blind to the fact that all women are physically and sexually similar. It is not proper for a man to have carnal affairs with more than one woman.

A MAN MUST NOT COPULATE WITH HIS WIFE during her period of menstruation. Indulging in copulation during this period will decrease the duration of his life.

SAGACIOUS PEOPLE NEVER ACT UPON A woman's advice. Women are the cause of all domestic disputes. They are also solely responsible for instigating all felonious wars and sinful deeds. This is why saintly people refrain from even viewing the reflection of a woman.

A WOMAN IN POSSESSION OF DESIRABLE womanly qualities will serve a man as a mother in the hours of dawn, and be as affectionate as a sister during the day. As the day turns into night, she metamorphosises into the perfect mistress to please him sexually. Such a woman will satisfy her husbands needs completely, and she will gain his trust. It is immaterial whether she is captivating or ugly, for she has the power to control her husband in all possible ways.

On Friendship

A MAN MAY BEHAVE PLEASANTLY IN YOUR presence, and yet curse you silently. Such a man does not deserve your friendship. Nurturing a relationship with such a man would be equivalent to chopping your feet off with your own axe. Such a friend is far more dangerous than an obvious enemy.

DO NOT SEEK THE COMPANY OF A MAN who derives pleasure from severing one's roots. Befriend a trustworthy man, who will exult in one's happiness, and prove to be a great support in times of trouble. But even to such a friend, one must not disclose these secrets, for when seized by annoyance, he may disclose one's secrets to one's enemies. Hence, one has to be very careful in shaping one's friendships.

ONE MUST ALWAYS SEEK TO BEFRIEND A person who possesses the qualities of brilliance, respect, fear, shame, and a sense of sacrifice. If these virtues do not exist in a person's heart, then he is not worthy of one's friendship. One can rest assured that such a friendship will not stand the test of time.

ONE MUST ESTABLISH A RAPPORT WITH A MAN who enjoys an equal status and position in society. When two people do not enjoy the same status, it is difficult for the friendship to run smoothly along parallel tracks. Sooner or later, dissension will set in, bringing the friendship to an abrupt end.

WHEN A MAN IS AFFLUENT, THERE WILL BE many people crowding around him. Under the guise of friendship, they all connive to fulfil their personal needs at his expense. The prosperous man is flattered by their show of adulation, but remains unaware of their true intent.

IT IS MAN'S SELFISHNESS THAT LEADS HIM INTO friendships. If one was not selfish, one would not feel the need to befriend others. That is the bitter truth.

A FRIEND'S SINCERITY CAN BE TESTED ONLY when one is in troubled waters. As long as there is happiness in one's home, people will staunchly stand by one. But a true friend will continue to stand by one, even in the face of a calamity.

A FRIEND IN NEED IS A FRIEND INDEED. A TRUE and sincere friend will protect you from all possible dangers. Friendship is held in even greater esteem than a sense of fraternity.

THERE CAN BE NO PEACE OR UNDERSTANDING between the snake and the mongoose, the goat and the tiger, or the lioness and the dog. Similiarly, it is not possible for the sinner and the saint to come to a friendly understanding. If such a friendship exists, it must be superficial and hypocritical. In a nutshell, a true friendship is not possible between persons with contrasting temperaments.

ONE MUST BE ABLE TO HAVE FAITH IN A FRIEND. A rapport with a feeble-minded man is far more dangerous than enmity with a mighty one. A feeble-minded man, with his inherent cowardice, will never be able to prove faithful to one.

JUST AS A MIRROR REFLECTS A MANS FACE, HIS personality is reflected in his choice of friends. One must always be careful in forming friendships and acquaintances, for one's friends, are in a way, an extension of one's inner inclinations and tendencies.

ONE SHOULD ALWAYS STEER CLEAR OF IDIOTS, for they are incapable of behaving like ordinary human beings. They are extremely loquacious and unpredictable, and they chatter without any sense of propriety. A wise man refrains from befriending an idiot, and never gives him refuge.

IF A PERSON, WILL SHED HIS BLOOD FOR YOUR sake, as unhesitatingly as he sheds his own sweat, only then should he be called your friend. Otherwise your friendship is nothing but sheer hypocrisy.

ANY INDIVIDUAL WHO ATTEMPTS TO ESTABLISH a sexual relationship with a woman from his friend's family, should be regarded as an absolutely depraved person.

THE TIES OF FRIENDSHIP THAT BOUND KRISHNA to Sudama; Arjuna to Krishna; and Rama to Vibhishana, were of an exemplary nature. Only such rare friendships are worthy of imitation.

A SAGACIOUS MAN GRAVELY CONSIDERS EACH friendship he cultivates. He knows that the seeds of friendship sown in haste will lay the ground for future animosity.

WHEN THE SON MATURES INTO AN ADULT, THE father must treat him like a friend.

IT IS MORE PLEASURABLE TO NURTURE A friendship with a young damsel, than to enter into a nuptial agreement with her. The irony of the matter is that it is only after various experiences in life, that one finally stumbles upon this realisation.

On Family

IF A MAN CAN DISCRIMINATE BETWEEN VICE and virtue, and judiciously weigh the pros and cons of an action, prior to its execution, then he will live a life of happiness. He will only have to face nominal suffering.

IF A MAN HAS A PUGNACIOUS WIFE, A DEVILISH friend, and an argumentative servant, and if a snake dwells in his home, then his is an accursed abode. In such a house, death could manifest itself at any moment.

A SINCERE FAMILY MEMBER ALWAYS FORESEES imminent danger from foes. He unhesitatingly employs all his physical, mental and financial strengths, and works zealously towards helping his family.

IF A MAN'S SON IS LOYAL TO HIM, AND HIS WIFE is a faithful woman, content with her husband's earnings, then his family will be blessed by the grace of God. If all the members of a family live with mutual fellow-feeling, then that family should be regarded as a peerless one.

A MAN MAY SUFFER ON NUMEROUS GROUNDS. It is quite likely that his lack of intellect will agonize him. He may also suffer anguish on account of the imprudent decisions, that he was goaded into making in his youth. But these sufferings are minimal, compared to the agony, of living with another's family. In a nutshell, it is most agonising and embarrasing to live with a family, that is not one's own.

A WISE MAN WILL ALWAYS TEACH HIS SONS about the nobility of moral codes. Once they have acquired a thorough knowledge of the Scriptures and morality, these sparkling gems will bring immortal fame to their ancestry.

IT IS THE FIRST AND FOREMOST DUTY OF parents to provide their children with an excellent education. Those parents who fail to do so, are their children's worst enemies. Uneducated children will always stand out as objects of ridicule in the company of those who are sagacious. They will look as awkward as herons among swans.

TOO MUCH PARENTAL AFFECTION WILL encourage vices in children. But firm and unyielding behaviour from parents will nourish virtues. Hence, it is necessary to maintain strictness at home. Parents must lavish less love on sons and disciples. It is the duty of each father and master to keep strict control over his sons and disciples, by enforcing rigid discipline. This will make them virtuous souls.

CHILDREN ARE SIMILIAR TO CLAY. THE FORM they ultimately assume, will depend on how they were moulded in their youth.

THOUGH THERE ARE INNUMERABLE TREES IN the forest, the fragrance exuded by the flowers of a single tree is enough to perfume the woodland. Similiarly, though one may have only one virtuous son, his presence will exalt one's ancestry to glorious heights.

ONLY A SINGLE TREE IN THE FOREST NEED BE ablaze, to start a forest fire. The entire forest will be consumed by flames. Similiarly if one of the descendants of a family chooses to live a wicked and licentious life, the reputation of the family will be destroyed in one fell swoop, and the entire clan will be wiped out.

WHY DO YOU CRAVE FOR MORE SONS? IF one of your sons stands tall as a model of righteousness, then the whole clan can depend on his virtue and strength.

ONE'S OFFSPRING SHOULD BE LOVED generously upto the age of five. For the next ten years, one should exercise strict control over them. When they reach the age of sixteen, one must treat them as one's friends.

PROSPERITY ABIDES ONLY IN THOSE FAMILIES, where debased individuals are neither entertained nor worshipped; where eatables remain preserved; and where there is a perfect consensus of opinion between husband and wife. Laxmi, (the Goddess of wealth) makes her abode only in such ideal homes.

AN ACCOMPLISHED AND VIRTUOUS SON, IS A thousand times better than a hundred foolish sons. The night sky is illuminated by the moon and the stars. But the millions of stars just cannot match the majestic splendour of the moon, as it lights up the dark heavens.

ONE FEELS LITTLE SORROW SEEING THE DEAD face of a depraved son. The bereavement will fade from one's memory with the passage of time. On the contrary, if he had been alive, he would have been a distressing presence in one's life.

IF A SON IS NEITHER LEARNED, NOR A DEVOTEE of the Lord, then he is the equivalent of a cow that can neither produce milk, nor proceed to a state of pregnancy.

THOUGH THEY ARE DIAMETRICALLY OPPOSITE in nature, the sweet plum and the prickly thorn, are borne by the same branch. Similiarly, a mother may give birth to twin sons, but despite the fact that they are born under the same celestial constellation, their conduct and demeanour are bound to be different.

A MAN MUST GIVE PATERNAL STATUS TO FIVE persons in his life. Firstly, to the one who sired him; secondly, to his consecrator; thirdly, to his instructor; fourthly, to his saviour in a perilious situation; and lastly, to his employer, whom he serves to earn his livelihood.

A FATHER PLUNGED IN DEBT, AN ADULTEROUS mother, a coquettish wife, and a quarrelsome son are determintal to the well-being of the family.

MERELY BELONGING TO A ILLUSTRIOUS LINEAGE will not bring one any honour. Even if a man has descended from an inferior family, if he is erudite and accomplished, then he deserves to be honoured.

STUDENTS MUST KEEP AWAY FROM THE following things: Lust, anger, greed, flavoured food, undue flamboyance, merry-making, excessive sleep and servitude. Only if they abstain from these evils, can they whole-heartedly devote themselves to their studies.

IF ONE HAS AN AFFECTIONATE WIFE, A LEARNED son, and one is prosperous and hospitable, then one is a blessed man.

IF ONE IS A DEVOTEE OF LORD SHIVA, WHO accompanies religious men on their journeys, and one has obedient servants, who serve a magnificent spread, then one has a blessed home.

A FAMILY IN WHICH THE WIFE IS ACCOMPLISHED, and the son is humble, is on par with Inderlok.

> *"I SHALL EXPOUND ON SUCH MORAL PRECEPTS in my scriptures. If one acts upon these, one can manage one's family affairs, wisely and well."*
>
> —Chanakya

On Spirituality

I SALUTE LORD VISHNU, THE PRESERVER OF THE three worlds.

I HAVE GARNERED ALL MY WORDLY WISDOM from the religious scriptures, and I write for the benefit of mankind at large. May Lord Vishnu aid me on this journey of enlightenment. May he grant me the capability and authority to put my knowledge to good use, so that my tasks may be accomplished.

EVERYDAY FOR AT LEAST HALF AN HOUR I WILL contemplate upon a few lines that I have authored. May God grant me the strength and wisdom to channelise all my efforts towards the study of the scriptures, religious activity and charity.

LIFE IS A PRICELESS OPPORTUNITY THAT God has granted one. Robust health is a blessing that must be fully appreciated. Before one's death, one must do something meritorious, both, for one's benefit, and for the benefit of mankind. The icy grip of Death will leave one totally paralysed and helpless. One can never control Fate.

CERTAIN PEOPLE HOLD AGNI (FIRE) TO be the most sacred God. Others see their God in stone idols, and therefore worship them. But one who is blessed with unprejudiced vision sees God in each particle of dust around him. Such wise men feel God's virtue, wherever they go.

MAN IS A FICKLE CREATURE. ALL HIS relationships are fleeting; all earthly prosperity is transient. Life is here today, and gone tomorrow. In such an unstable world, Only Truth is indestructible. Only Truth is eternal. Everything else is illusory. Let this be emblazoned on your mind. Always perform your duty, and act in accordance with the ethical principles laid down in the holy scriptures.

IF ONE WISHES TO BE EMANCIPATED AND erudite, then one must acquire listening skills. Only through listening can one come upon Truth, and knowledge of the Self. A listener will abandon all evil. Through listening one acquires immense power. It exerts a positive influence on one's temperament.

ONE'S LIFE IS PRE-ORDAINED. WHATEVER will be, will be. Destiny exercises powerful control over a man's intellect and behaviour. His stars govern and influence his life. Nobody is liable for the course that another's life may take. It is written in the stars.

EVEN ALMIGHTY GOD IS HELPLESS BEFORE certain natural phenomena. Everything on earth is governed by the infallible laws of Nature. Even God adheres to these laws.

ALL THE HAPPENINGS ON EARTH ARE ACTS OF Providence. Brahma has the power to convert a beggar into a king, and a king into a beggar.

I CAN PROCLAIM CONFIDENTLY THAT Hari (God) is the preserver of life. That is why I am quiet and unruffled. The birth of a child is probably the greatest proof of God's existence. There is milk for him in his mother's breast, even before he has been placed in the haven of her arms. What a marvel! My Salutations to the Lord!

AS LONG AS HIS BLESSINGS ARE UPON US, we can live without fear and worry.

TWO THOUSAND FIVE HUNDRED YEARS INTO Kaliyuga, Apollyon's influence will rob men of their virtues.

Anarchy will prevail Five thousand years into Kaliyuga, the sacred Ganges will be parched. After ten thousand years, Lord Vishnu will forsake Mother Earth. The Devil will rule and the world will face Doomsday. Only after destruction can a purer world be created. This cycle will repeat itself endlessly.

IF ONE'S HEART IS TAINTED BY IMMORALITY AND sin, then one cannot profit from regular visits to pilgrim centres. The heart of a debauched man has no salvation. Whatever the means employed, a wine container can never be purified.

GOSSIPING DURING A MEAL IS STRICTLY forbidden. It is virtuous to maintain silence while eating. If, for an entire year, one observes silence during mealtimes, one will attain longevity and eternal bliss.

IF A MAN APPEASES THE HUNGER OF THE impoverished, and bestows alms to Brahmins, then God beholds his magnanimity, and blesses him generously.

A MAN WHO DOES NOT WORSHIP AT LORD Krishna's feet; who does not sing praises of the love of Radha and Krishna; and who does not know anecdotes from the Krishnaleela, is living a cursed life. Such a man will always be beset by worries. He will never gain Supreme Knowledge of the Self. He has not done justice to earthly life.

IF KADEEM'S TREE IS UNABLE TO BEAR LEAVES, should one blame the spring? Is the sun to blame for the owl's blindness during the day? Must one rebuke the clouds, if the chavak failed to enjoy the drops of rain? Accept acts of Providence. One cannot change that which is pre-ordained.

THE HUMAN BODY IS DESTRUCTIBLE. Affluence, too, is unreliable. Therefore, one should waste little time in earthly frivolities. One should perform virtuous deeds, and aim for a spiritual life, for therein lies true prosperity. A man's spiritual self will not only help him cope with earthly life, but will also guide him after death, into his next life.

A MAN CAN BE RESERVOIR OF VIRTUE. HE MAY possess many sterling qualities, but the basic question is, how to utilise these qualities for optimum benefit.

THE KALP TREE (WHICH IN HINDU MYTHOLOGY, fulfils all human desires), is just a product of wood. The Sameru mountain is nothing but an immovable dust heap. The Chintamani is a mere precious stone, and the Kamadhenu is just an animal. Lord Rama, you will always be peerless! Not even the sun and the oceans can compare to you.

THE AGE, PERSEVERANCE, KNOWLEDGE, education, prosperity and death of a man are determined by Nature, as he lies nestled in his mother's womb. Man is a mere puppet in the hands of Fate. He dances to Destiny's tune.

ONCE A MAN HAS ACQUIRED KNOWLEDGE OF the Self, his Ego just melts away. Subsequent to the destruction of the Ego, man transcends earthly life, and achieves oneness with the Supreme Being.

LIFE IS IRONICAL. MAN'S DESIRES REMAIN unfulfilled; his achievements remain unrealised. Since everything is in Kaamdev's (cupid) hands, one must learn to be content with one's lot. This is the sole way to achieve happiness.

THE DETACHMENT THAT ONE FEELS, LISTENING to one's spiritual guide, or seeing the cremation of a corpse is merely fleeting.

ONCE A MAN'S MIND IS DETACHED, HE CAN effortlessly transcend the world of extreme happiness and extreme suffering. He arrives at a state of beatitude, called Kaivalya.

MAN IS ENSLAVED BY HIS FIVE SENSORY ORGANS (eye, ear, nose, toungue and skin), and his Karmendriyas (i.e. hand, feet, mouth, penis, and anus). If a man wishes to go beyond earthly life, then he must gain full control over these senses. Once he manages to do so, he cultivates a spiritual identity that separates him from earthly life. This enables him to transcend birth and death.

IF ONE HAS A HEART WHICH IS FULL OF compassion for one's fellow beings, then there is no need to grow one's hair and smear ash on one's body, like a Sadhu.

IF A MAN IS SLOTHFUL, UNHYGIENIC, AND profane, then Laxmi, the Goddess of Wealth will most certainly forsake him.

THE SPOON THAT STIRS THE DELICIOUS FOOD, remains unaware of its taste. Similiarly, a man who goes through the Scriptures, without any apparent diligence or devotion, will never know Eternal Truth.

5

Observations On Everyday Life

IF A TOWN IS INHABITED BY FOOLS, WHO DO not know how to respect others, then one must forsake it. Also, if a town offers no source of livehood or friendship; if there is no institution that imparts education; if there are neither doctors, nor men of learning or affluence; then it should be abandoned, as a town not worthy of settling in.

KNOWLEDGE IN A MAN, BORN INTO AN INFERIOR family, and cultured manners in a girl, with an infamous ancestry, should be accepted, as unhesitatingly, as poison found in elixir, or gold discovered in an unsanctified place.

ONE MUST BE SECRETIVE. TAKE THE UTMOST care not to reveal one's heart to others. One must always act, after having carefully pondered over the blunders one has committed in the past. To succeed in this world of competition and rivalry, the virtue of secretiveness has to be acquired.

AN ASTUTE MAN MARRIES HIS DAUGHTER INTO a family with a noble, and illustrious ancestry. He provides his son with the best education, religionizes his friend, and entangles his enemy in a messy situation. A man who fulfils all these duties, can be assured of a happy and meritorious life.

DILIGENCE PUTS AN END TO ONE'S PENURY. THE company of noble men and saints keeps one away from sin. Taciturnity helps one avoid unnecessary hostility. Constant alertness enables one to overcome fear.

HOUSEHOLDERS ALWAYS TRY TO STEER THEIR sons away from hermits and spiritual persons, proficient in the Scriptures and Vedas. They labour under the misapprehension that the company of such men may bring about a streak of renunciation in their sons. But only the society of such men will make their sons paragons of virtue. The eminence of these men will never be forgotten. It will live on, to be enjoyed by their descendants.

HOW AM I PASSING MY TIME? WHO ARE MY friends and enemies? Which country am I a citizen of? Which clan do I owe allegiance to? What are my gains or losses in my endeavours? A man must always ponder over these questions, for in their answers lies his destiny, and his key to worldly success.

A PRUDENT MAN IS ALWAYS ON THE ALERT FOR problems that may manifest themselves in the future. As a result, he is always equipped to meet them. The simpleton who behaves without any foresight, is forced to suffer the consequences.

ONE SHOULD NOT BE ALARMED AT THE SIGHT of misfortune on a distant horizon. Should one see calamity approaching swiftly, then one must face it fearlessly.

AN AFFLUENT MAN'S RELATIVES WILL constantly flock around him. Nobody will approach a pauper. A prosperous man must always take care to avoid those relatives, who are conniving with each other to rob him of his wealth. An affluent man is always befooled by others into believing that he is a wise man. He should always be conscious of people's attempts to deceive him.

He should save his money, and refrain from extravagance.

THE LION, KING OF THE ANIMALS, HAS ONE outstanding virtue. He puts his heart into every activity he undertakes. Whatever he does, he does with vigour. Every deed is executed with total commitment, devotion and single-minded intensity.

A HERON POSSESSES THE VIRTUES OF SELF-restraint, flexibility, (it adjusts its behaviour according to the need of the moment), and foresight.

THE COCK RISES AT THE CRACK OF DAWN. HE IS always ready to fight and chase away his rivals. He also has the habit of snatching away others' food.

A DOG IS CONTENT WITH WHATEVER HE GETS. He is complacent, even when he begins to experience the pangs of hunger. He is brave and faithful. A dog is alert even in sleep. These are his outstanding virtues.

THE CROW HOARDS FOOD FROM TIME TO TIME, and takes care not to trust anybody. He behaves with utmost circumspection. Moreover, a crow only copulates occasionally.

THE DONKEY WORKS VIGOUROUSLY, EVEN when his limbs are weary. He cultivates an indifference to the scorching summer heat, and this enables him to plod on relentless of his exhaustion. Come what may, he is always tranquil and content. This is an admirable quality.

IF ONE MAKES A SINCERE ATTEMPT TO ACQUIRE all the qualities narrated above, then success is inevitable.

IF A MAN MAKES SINCERE EFFORTS TO AMASS knowledge; unhesitatingly interchanges food and money; and firmly believes in mutual give and take, then he will always be happy.

A MAN WHO CONSTANTLY HANKERS AFTER wealth, will never attain the happiness of the man, who is content with what he has.

ONE MUST ALWAYS BE CONTENT WITH ONE'S wife, one's supply of food and one's wealth.

INITIALLY, ONE'S ENEMY SHOULD BE HANDLED in accordance with the ethical code. He should be approached submissively, and every effort must be made to appease his animosity. Yet, if despite sincere efforts at conciliation, the evil enemy maintains his hostile stance, then one should prepare to handle him with the necessary cunning. He must be crushed ruthlessly.

IN THE FOREST, ONLY THOSE TREES WITH curved trunks escape the woodcutter's axe. The trees that stand straight and tall, fall to the ground. This only illustrates that it is not too advisable to live in this world as an innocent, modest man.

SWANS ARE KNOWN TO SHIFT REPEATEDLY from their place of dwelling. They forsake parched ponds for places where drinking water is available in plenty. However, it is important that Man does not imitate this particular trait of the swan, as this could bring about disorder and chaos in his life.

A YAVAN (GREEK CITIZEN) IS THE EMBODIMENT of sin and licentiousness. But this fact is only apparent to a man of substance – one who is shrewd and unprejudiced.

ONE MUST BATHE AFTER COPULATING; massaging with oil; shaving off one's hair or beard; and inhaling the fumes from the funeral pyre. If one fails to do so, one remains unsanctified.

IF ONE DRINKS WATER, AFTER ONE HAS digested one's food, then water will have the quality of ambrosia. But, if one drinks water before digesting one's meal, then water will have a toxic effect. Drinking water immediately after a meal could prove to be injurious to health.

A FEW THINGS ONE SHOULD ALWAYS KEEP IN mind:

- Gurch, (a parasitic creeper) is one of the most useful medicines.
- A substantial meal gives one the greatest possible happiness.
- The head rules the body, but sight takes precedence over all other senses.

•

ANYTHING THAT MAN DOES INDEPENDENTLY, indicates his superiority. If one makes one's own beaded garland, rubs one's own sandal paste, and composes one's own hymns, they will be a class apart. They will also bring one immense joy and gratification. Dependence makes a man inferior in his own eyes. All kinds of dependence should be discouraged. One must be self-reliant.

SOIL, SUGAR-CANE, SESAMUM, SANDAL WOOD and gold will exhibit their inherent worth, only when they are crushed and ground repeatedly.

WITH PATIENCE AND DILIGENCE, EVEN POVERTY can be transformed into affluence. Brisk, vigorous cleaning will remove dirt, and successfully transform an unsightly home into a beautiful one. This is similar to cooking raw vegetables to lend them flavour and spice.

ONE MUST ALWAYS REMEMBER TO GIVE careful consideration to each deed. Each step must be taken with great caution. One must take care to behave sagaciously in the society of men; speak as instructed in the scriptures; and drink only filtered water.

KNOWLEDGE AND WISDOM WILL FORSAKE THE one who pursues worldly pleasure, luxury, and sensuality. One who aspires to acquire scriptural knowledge, must not attach any weight to such frivolous things. The convergence of the worldly and saintly life is as illusory as the convergence of the earth and sky on the horizon.

KNOWLEDGE CAN BE ATTAINED, ONLY AFTER A laborious and persistent effort.

FLOUR POSSESSES TEN TIMES MORE ENERGY than grain; milk possesses ten times more energy than flour; meat possesses ten times more energy than milk; ghee possesses ten times more energy than meat.

MILK LENDS ONE ENERGY, GHEE THICKENS one's semen, and meat fattens one's body.

BEREAVEMENT CAN BRING ABOUT PHYSICAL AND psychological illnesses.

ONE, WHO IS MAGNANIMOUS WITH HIS FAMILY; sympathetic to others; rigidly opposed to the wicked; and respectful and humble in the company of saints and savants, is the wisest of men.

ONE WHO IS BRAVE BEFORE HIS ENEMIES; complacent before his elders; astute with women; and self-centred in his dealings with the crafty and cunning, will always be happy. He will never trespass the limits of decency.

IF A MAN SPENDS EXTRAVAGANTLY WITHOUT foresight, and tends to be parasitic, quarrelsome, and ever ready to enter into a sexual relationship with woman, irrespective of her caste, creed or religion, then he will surely meet with an untimely death.

IF A MAN IS ALWAYS RECEPTIVE TO MORE knowledge and education; unhesitant in accepting food from others; and strongly inclined to share everything that he has, then he will live a calm, quiet and fulfilling life.

ONE CANNOT CHANGE THE PAST, BUT ONE CAN ruin a perfectly good present by worrying about the future. The past is irrevocable, and the future is totally unpredictable. Only the present exists, so one should think of today. If one treads the path of the present, then one will touch the peaks of happiness.

BLIND ATTACHMENT AND INFATUATION WILL only cause suffering, pain, anxiety and fear. That is why, wise men never commit the folly of getting attached to people. Thus, they remain in a state of bliss.

IF A MAN HAS THE FORESIGHT AND WISDOM TO seek the remedies for imminent hazards, and he is prepared to face the world squarely, then he will move fearlessly through life. A blunt fatalist, who believes that everything is governed by some unknown power called God, deadens himself before his death. His attitude deprives him of his brilliance and vitality, and renders him soulless.

ONE'S MIND IS RESPONSIBLE, BOTH FOR ONE'S worldly bondage, and liberation from material life. An attached mind is inclined towards earthly objects. A detached mind is indifferent to them. Bondage is when one's mind is enmeshed in worldly life. The ultimate emancipation, is when one's mind soars above earthly pleasures.

IF A MAN IS FICKLE AND INDECISIVE, THEN HE can never taste happiness. A life of isolation in a forest will make him crave for human company; a life in the society of men will baffle him. Neither of these alternatives can bring him lasting joy. Such a man will always be burdened by his discontent.

WHEN THE EARTH IS DUG UP WITH A HOE, THE water gushes to the surface. Similiarly, if the disciple serves his master with unconditional love and faith, he is sure to gain wisdom and knowledge of the Self.

IT IS TRUE THAT, AS A MAN SOWS, SO SHALL HE reap. A man's destiny is governed solely by his actions. He, who is astute and perceptive, will always think carefully before carrying out an action.

IF A MAN, WHO HAS LEARNT EVEN A LETTER from a Master, behaves in an ungrateful manner, he will face unending suffering. He will be reborn into a family with a criminal lineage. A man must always feel highly indebted to his master.

IT IS ONLY A KNOWLEDGE OF THE WORLD AND self-awareness that distinguishes man from animal – for an animal too, eats, sleeps, copulates and feels fear. Therefore, a man without knowledge, is in no way superior to an animal.

IF A MAN'S HEART IS FULL OF MAGNANIMITY AND compassion towards his fellow human beings, he will attain worldly prosperity, as he moves through life. All his problems will be solved of their own accord.

EVEN THAT, WHICH IS UNATTAINABLE THROUGH effort, is attainable through a life of austerity. An austere life is even mightier than a forceful effort.

A MAN MUST OPEN-HEARTEDLY ACCEPT TWO things in life. Firstly, erudition, and secondly, the company of noble, virtuous people. Those men, who earnestly aspire to be happy and prosperous will always seek the company of noble ones.

IN ORDER TO PLEASE OTHERS, ONE MUST always use mellifluent language. Speaking in a charming and pleasant manner does not cost one anything.

BETRAYING A FRIEND; TAKING SHELTER IN THE enemy camp; and adopting illegal measures to obtain money, is not acceptable, even in days of adversity. The money earned employing illegal means is ignoble and contemptible.

IF ONE HAS EARNED MONEY BY ADOPTING unjustified means, then it will remain with one for ten years. In the eleventh year, such undeserved wealth is not only destroyed, but also serves as one's nemesis. One must always keep this in view. Take care never to employ illegal measures to earn money!

EVEN IF THE MASTER HAS PREACHED ONLY A single word to his disciple, he deserves his reverence. The act of preaching or imparting knowledge is not only the noblest of all acts, but also a favour that can never be repaid.

BEFORE DOING ANY DEED, ONE SHOULD ALWAYS ponder over its consequences. If a deed should compel one to repent later, and atone for one's action, then it is not worth doing.

Before carrying out any action ask yourself three questions:

- Why am I doing this?
- What will be the consequences of this action?
- Will this exercise be a success, or a fiasco?

AFTER QUESTIONING ONESELF, ONE SHOULD ACT according to the conclusion one arrives at.

ONE SHOULD ONLY TRUST ONESELF. OFTEN, trusting others is futile and dangerous. They will not hesitate to lead us straight into the pit of treachery. One should always have confidence in oneself.

Aphorisms

IT IS PAINFUL TO WASTE ONE'S TIME, ADVISING a silly disciple, indulging a quarrelsome wife, and listening to other's tales of woe.

IF ONE CASTS ASIDE THAT WHICH CAN BE obtained, and pursues that, which is out of one's reach, then one will lose both the obtainable and the unobtainable.

NEVER TRUST RIVERS, WOMEN, DESCENDENTS of royal families, men with weapons, and animals endowed with horns and claws.

AN IDEAL SON IS OBEDIENT AND SINCERE. AN able father ensures that he is provided with an excellent education. An ideal friend is trustworthy, and an ideal wife will give her husband intense pleasure during intercourse.

AUTHENTIC JEWELS AND SANDALWOOD ARE not seen everywhere. Occasionally, they are found in rare places. True saints are equally hard to come by. The adage, "All that glitters is not gold" always holds good. There is too much artificiality in the world. One must be discerning to recognise that, which is authentic.

EVERYTHING IS SIGNIFICANT IN ITS OWN unique way. The King gives maximum importance to the welfare of his subjects. A Bania has only his business in mind. Knowledge is the only concern of an erudite man. A bewitching wife truly beautifies her house.

WHEN THE DEER SENSES A FOREST FIRE, HE IS quick to forsake the forest. Similiarly, once the Brahmin has accepted Dakshina (reward given to Brahmin after the rituals), he is quick to leave. Once the disciple has gleaned knowledge from the Master, he promptly takes his leave from him.

HE WHO IS STEEPED IN DEBT, DISHONOURED BY his own kith and kin, separated from his wife, and limited by wicked men, will experience terrible heartache.

THE TREE THAT GROWS ON THE RIVERBANK IS to be pitied. Similiarly, a woman who deserts her husband for another man, and a King who is without a judicious Minister, suffer a sorry plight.

A BRAHMIN'S WEALTH IS HIS KNOWLEDGE. A King's wealth is his army. A Vaishya's greatest asset is his wealth. A Sudra's asset is his service.

BIRDS DESERTS TREES WHICH ARE BARE; A prostitute abandons a poor, destitute man; and subjects abandon a powerless king. This always holds true.

PURE HAPPINESS IS JUST IMPOSSIBLE ON EARTH. There is no clan which is free of particular moral frailties.

One's physical stamina is constantly threatened by disease. Suffering will also dog one like an inseparable shadow.

ONE'S BEHAVIOUR WILL REVEAL WHICH CLAN one has descended from. One's speech will reveal one's nationality. One's respect for others reflects the measure of grace and love in one's heart. One's body mirrors the kind of food one consumes.

SAINTLY MEN ARE TOTALLY TRUSTWORTHY. ONE need never fear their betrayal. Therefore, kings enjoy accompanying them on their journeys.

THOUGH THE OCEAN IS ALMOST ALWAYS tranquil, a great storm can whip up the waves, and cause a devastating flood. But, however piqued and insulted a saintly man may feel, when faced with unjust criticism, he will never rise to the bait, and cross the limits of decency.

A NIGHTINGALE'S GREATEST ASSET IS ITS melodious voice. A woman's greatest asset is her fidelity. A man's power lies in his knowledge. A sage's glory lies in his ability to forgive folly.

ONE MUST BE READY TO RENOUNCE ONE'S family, village, nation, and even the world, for the sake of one's self-respect.

ALL EXCESSES ARE HAZARDOUS. SITA, THE IDEAL wife and companion, was abducted by Ravana. Ravana's terrible self-conceit led to the devastation of his whole clan. Bali's excessively charitable nature led him to bondage.

ONCE A MAN'S AMBITION IS KINDLED, NOTHING can stop *him.* For a businessman, no country can be too far. For a wise man, there is no such thing as a foreign land. He is at home wherever he goes.

THE COMPANY OF SAINTLY PERSONS, NURTURES virtues in human beings. Their proximity is always a source of great delight.

A PEEVISH WIFE, A FOOLISH SON, AND A WIDOW in the house, can really incense a man. Serving a depraved clan, and residing in the vicinity of a quarrelsome man, will also raise a man's wrath. He will be ablaze with passionate fury.

AFTER THE AGONY OF WORLDLY EXISTENCE, in old age, one finds peace and comfort in the affection of one's offspring, the companionship of one's wife, and the proximity of saints.

THREE THINGS SHOULD NEVER BE REPEATED: A King's decree; an erudite man's statement; and Kanyadaan (when a bride is entrusted to her husband by her father).

AUSTERITIES MUST ALWAYS BE PRACTISED IN solitude. But one should always study in the company of another; sing, accompanied by two people; travel, in the company of three others; foster ties with at least four persons; and wage wars with the aid of innumerable soldiers. This advice will prove advantageous to one in the long run.

A HOUSE WITHOUT CHILDREN WILL WEAR A

deserted look.

Sans company, a journey will be lonely and directionless. Gloom will prevail in a impoverished man's life, and he will drown in his despondency. An ignorant man is fated to live his life in disgrace.

ONE MUST ALWAYS FORSAKE A PEEVISH WIFE, disrespectful brothers, a master, who is neither wise nor erudite, and the religion which does not practice mercy.

UNDIGESTED FOOD WILL BRING ABOUT physical maladies; the company of the poor will make one look weary; and the marriage of an old man to a young lady will result in sexual dissatisfaction, conflict and estrangement.

IF ONE'S KNOWLEDGE OF THE SCRIPTURES IS not put into practice, then the years of study will have gone to waste.

FIRE IS TREATED MOST REVERENTIALLY BY THE Brahmin (an enlightened man), the Kshatriya (the warrior), and the Vaishya.

ONE MUST ALWAYS BEAR IN MIND THAT A GUEST in one's house must be treated with immense reverence. Also, a woman should always treat her husband with great respect.

IF A MAN IS INCLINED TOWARDS THE SPIRITUAL, then he will be unable to attain success in earthly life. If a man does not crave for carnal pleasure, then he will waste little time preening himself. A wise man will never be able to deliver a speech, that is to the liking of the common man. A straightforward man is virtually incapable of being crafty in his dealings with others.

ENVY IS A NATIVE INSTINCT OF MAN. THE stupid will envy the sapient; the poor will envy the affluent; the prostitute will envy the noble woman; and the widow will envy the woman, whose husband is alive.

INDOLENCE WILL DEFINITELY DESTROY A MAN'S knowledge. But a well-balanced diet, and controlled passion can effectively protect it. It is the kindness of subjects that protects a King. The cultured, and well-mannered wife protects the house. It is the abscence of a forceful general that leads to the army's defeat.

ONE WHO VILLIFIES A LEARNED AND DEEPLY content man for no apparent reason, will suffer a great deal because of his wicked Karma.

CHARITY REMOVES POVERTY. AMIABILITY AND equanimity will put an end to all kinds of suffering. A sharp intellect will dispel the darkness of one's ignorance, and noble intentions will blot out all fear from our minds.

A MAN INFLICTED BY SENSUALITY IS A SPIRITUAL pauper. He is physically feeble, perverted and dull.

ONE'S IGNORANCE IS ONE'S MOST POWERFUL enemy. One's anger will scorch the very core of one's heart. It is even more powerful than fire. The attainment of knowledge and wisdom is the greatest happiness that one can experience.

NO MAN CAN ESCAPE THE CONSEQUENCES OF his actions. One's actions will chase one like a persistent shadow. One creates one's own heaven or hell. Ultimately, emancipation can be attained only through rigorous effort and penance.

FOR AN ENLIGHTENED MAN, HEAVEN HAS little value. If a man is belligerent, then life itself will be meaningless. A sensuous woman will have little effect on a man who exercises rigid control over his senses.

ONLY MAN'S KARMA WILL GUIDE HIM AFTER HE has abandoned earthly life. Good Karma is like medicine given to the ailing man; like knowledge for the ignorant soul.

THE EXPANSE OF THE OCEAN WILL NOT GAIN from a little rain. Food cannot further satisfy one who has eaten a full meal. A wealthy man will not profit from charity.

THE RAIN CLOUD IS THE MOST SACRED SOURCE of water. The greatest task is that, which is conscientiously and indefatigably accomplished. The splendour of the eyes will remain unmatched by all the wonders of the world.

THE IMPOVERISHED SOULS, WHO EXPERIENCE the agony of poverty, yearn for prosperity. Animals crave for the power of speech. While mortals crave the comforts of heaven, celestial deities long for final beatitude. It is a long, hard path to that state of being, where one is devoid of desire.

IT IS VIRTUALLY IMPOSSIBLE TO SEE THROUGH the hearts of the crow, the jackal, the barber, and the gardener's wife. They are extremely clever and crafty. It is very difficult to know what goes on in their minds.

THOSE WHO POSE AS SAINTS, WHILE SECRETLY behaving in an irreligious and ignoble manner, are contemptible creatures. But those men who slander others, and spread malicious rumours about them, are the meanest creatures on this planet.

WHEREAS A BRONZE POT IS CLEANED USING ash, tamarind is employed to clean a copper pot. A woman is considered pure after menstruation. A river is cleansed of its filth by the rapid and unobstructed flow of water.

A KING, A BRAHMIN, AND A YOGI WHO HAVE A yen for travel, will be widely respected. By indulging their wanderlust, they enrich the lives of innumerable people. But a woman with a passion for travel, will never be considered honourable. She will be looked down upon; people will always eye her with scorn and suspicion.

The Essential Precepts

CLOUDED VISION

A MAN CAN BE POSSESSED BY VARIOUS KINDS OF blindness. Some, unfortunately, are born blind. There are others who have been blessed with vision, but owing to various reasons, they are blind to life around them. Such men are not blind – they are blindfolded.

IF A MAN IS BLINDED IN THE MONTH OF SAAWAN, then his vision is obscured by fallacious and pre-possessed notions. Such men are shorn of the virtue of unprejudiced perception.

OTHERS ARE BLINDED BY SEX, GREED AND inebriety. These people are so blinded by their vices, that they are incapable of seeing things as they are. Their perception is clouded to such an extent, that they seem oblivious to the hell they have created for themselves. They stumble through life like blind men.

EXPLOITATION

IF ONE WISHES TO FULFIL ONE'S ENDS, IT IS important to keep the likes, dislikes, prejudices, unclinations and weaknesses of others in mind.

FLASH MONEY BEFORE THE GREEDY MAN; BE respectful to the egoist; keep up a pretence of truthfulness before the wise man; and allow the imbecile to behave as he wishes to.

IF ONE BEHAVES IN THE ABOVE-MENTIONED ways, one's prey becomes vulnerable to exploitation.

THE COMPANY OF THE IGNOBLE

HOW CAN ONE PROFIT FROM THE COMPANY OF ignoble men?

SUBJECTS DERIVE LITTLE BENEFIT FROM A KING who is a reprobate and a tyrant.

IT DOES NOT PROFIT ONE TO BE IN THE company of a friend who secretly nurses treacherous thoughts in his heart. He could stab one in the back at any moment.

A WICKED AND INSINCERE DISCIPLE CANNOT enhance the master's reputation in any way. A disciple who will veer from the path of truth, does not deserve to be initiated. He will never be able to expound his master's teachings.

THERE IS NO SATISFACTION TO BE DERIVED from entering into a marriage with a quarrelsome and adulterous woman. One's life will become a living hell, devoid of peace and harmony.

A LIFE OF SECLUSION IS PREFERABLE TO THE company of ignoble men. A degenerate king, a treacherous friend, an insincere disciple, and an adulterous woman, can only get one into a scrape. There is little to be gained from their company.

ON INTERFERENCE

ONE MUST NOT INTERVENE IN OTHER'S AFFAIRS.

NEVER RAISE THE WRATH OF A BRAHMIN, FOR he is liable to curse you. Similiarly, one must never come between a husband and wife, or a master and servant. It could result in profound embarassment.

ALSO, SHOULD ONE PLAY WITH FIRE, OR attempt to pass through the yoke of the oxen and plough, – it could result in fatal injuries.

SACRED ENTITIES

FIRE, A BRAHMIN, A VIRGIN GIRL, AN OLD MAN, and a child, are all equally sacred. One must never touch them with one's foot.

FIRE WILL DOUBTLESS BURN YOU.

A BRAHMIN AND AN OLDER MAN WILL BE SURE to express their displeasure.

THE VIRGIN GIRL AND THE CHILD ARE THE VERY embodiments of God.

REMEMBER THAT ANYONE WHO IS ELDER TO one, and possesses superior knowledge, deserve one's reverence.

FOREWARNED IS FOREARMED

ONE SHOULD STAY AT LEAST A THOUSAND FEET away from an elephant, a hundred feet away from a horse, and ten feet away from any animal with horns. If one keeps a distance from the above mentioned animals, one can learn a great deal about their intentions and their aggression.

IF ONE SHOULD ENCOUNTER A WICKED PERSON, then one must immediately take to one's heels. A villain can attack from any distance. Moreover, such a man will never reveal his true intentions to anyone.

THE CONDUCT MERITS THE TREATMENT

AN ELEPHANT MUST BE CONTROLLED USING AN ankush (iron hook); a horse using a whip; and a horned animal, with the aid of a cudgel. But an evil man must never be spared the sword, he must have rigorous punishment enforced on him. This is the only way to keep him under control. Therefore the saying, "the conduct merits the treatment."

AN IMMUTABLE TEMPERAMENT

EACH INDIVIDUAL ON EARTH, POSSESSES HIS own unique temperament. The temperament determines all his joys and sorrows.

A BRAHMIN'S HAPPINESS LIES IN WITNESSING other's joy. The sight of delicious food being laid out before him, and the sound of the rolling clouds of thunder, evoke strong feelings of joy in him.

ON THE CONTRARY, AN EVIL PERSON'S DELIGHT lies in another's distress. He is happy witnessing another's suffering. He is similiar to a brier, for it is in the brier's nature to prick others. One can do little about this. People's temperaments will always remain immutable.

NO ONE IS WEAK

ALMIGHTY GOD HAS MADE EACH INDIVIDUAL mighty.

ONE WHO IS CONVERSANT IN THE VEDAS, AND has consequently attained a realisation of Self, is powerful in his own right. His power lies in his knowledge of the Scriptures and his Self-realisation.

AN ENCHANTRESS HAS THE POWER TO BEWITCH people. She has the ability to charm and fascinate those she encounters.

EACH INDIVIDUAL IS UNIQUELY POWERFUL AND competent. No-one should be regarded as weak or powerless. When a suitable opportunity arises, a man could dazzle you with an unexpected display of skill and power. Therefore, even an apparently weak enemy should never be written off as easily conquerable.

INFLUENCE OF ASSOCIATION

WHEN A DROP OF WATER FALLS ON A HEATED tavva, it makes a musical hiss before it evaporates into thin air.

WHEN A DROP OF WATER FALLS ON A LOTUS petal, it lies there, gleaming in the morning sun, and then gradually disappears.

WHEN A DROP OF WATER FALLS INTO THE mouth of a snake, especially in Swati-Nakshtra (fifteenth lunar mansion in the path of the Moon), it is transformed into a pearl.

THIS ILLUSTRATES THAT, OFTEN, IT IS THE company that determines the nature of things. The company that one keeps will undoubtedly exert a subtle influence on one's nature. One's company can control most of one's actions and intellectual decisions.

GLORY OF MONEY

MONEY WILL BRING ONE GREAT VENERATION and esteem. There will always be many friends buzzing around one, who is wealthy and prosperous. He becomes the centre of all attention. His brothers will idolise him as the epitome of dignity and respectability. Only a prosperous man, is treated like a "man" in the real sense of the word, and he lives as a man ideally should. An impoverished man crawls among the filth, in the lowest levels of society. Quite often, the faults of the affluent man, are overlooked by the people, for they hope that he will prove useful in the near or distant future. Therefore, even the erudite, sing praises of rich men, hoping to curry favour with them.

POVERTY IS A MALEDICTION THAT MUST BE staved off. One should endeavour to attain wealth and affluence.

DEITY IN THE FORM OF MAN

IF A MAN IS TRUE DEVOTEE OF THE LORD – IF he is charitable, soft-spoken, and hospitable to Brahmins – then the grace of God will be on his abode. Such a man is God Incarnate, and he deserves great veneration. Those men who possess these noble virtues are truly blessed.

DAMNED ONES

IF A MAN IS HOSTILE TOWARDS HIS OWN

friends and brothers; if his anger is uncontrollable, and his speech is fiery, then he will be condemned to eternal hell. Such antagonistic and fiendish people will experience hell on earth.

THE WAY OF LIVING

IN THE LION'S DEN, ONE CAN FIND AN elephant's skull and pieces of flesh.

IN A JACKAL'S LAIR, ONE CAN FIND THE TORN-out tail of a calf, along with a donkey's skin.

IF ONE IS CAREFUL TO OBSERVE THE THINGS scattered around in a house, one can roughly guess the nature of the man who dwells there. One's house mirrors one's way of living, and the inner quality of one's being.

EMINENCE OVER AFFLUENCE

MEAN-SPIRITED MEN, BORN INTO INFERIOR families, constantly hanker after money. For such men, wealth is the most precious thing in the world.

MEN OF AVERAGE INTELLIGENCE SEEK WEALTH, and simultaneously strive to attain honour and social respectability.

MEN, WHO HAIL FROM FAMILIES, BOASTING OF A

noble and distinguished lineage, desire only respect and glory. Such men give immense weightage to dignity and notability, and little importance to worldly riches.

ELIGIBILITY

MONEY MUST BE GIVEN AWAY ONLY TO MEN OF virtue. They are the only ones who truly-deserve it. The sea only lends its water to the clouds. The clouds transform this water into ambrosia. It rains down on earth and sea, replenishing life, and providing subsistence. It is also a refreshing stimulus for the creatures of the earth.

ONE MUST THINK CAREFULLY BEFORE GIVING away even a single paisa. Always take into account whom it is being given to.

PATRONAGE

KNOWLEDGE CANNOT BE ATTAINED WITHOUT diligence. Idleness will devastate the tree of knowledge, and once that occurs we will witness the annihilation of humanity. In the absence of the General, the army is shorn of its invincibility. After the death of the husband, life ceases to hold any charm for the wife. Her life stagnates like a pool of water. Similarly, in the abscence of tutelage, life loses all it's meaning.

MISFORTUNE

THERE ARE INNUMERABLE MOMENTS OF misfortune in one's life. But the death of one's wife in old age; seizure of one's ancestral property by one's brothers; insecurity about the availability of food; and dependence on others, are without doubt, the most unfortunate situations.

EARNEST DETERMINATION

AGNIHOTRA, (THE CEREMONY IN WHICH oblations are offered to the consecrated fire), is futile without a comprehensive study of the Vedas. Without proper knowledge, religious sacrifices will not yield the desired results. Without diligence and tenacity, it is almost impossible to attain perfection.

IN THE FIRST PLACE, EACH PURSUIT MUST BE given earnest consideration. Dedication and perserverance are also absolutely essential. Without these qualities, nothing substantial can ever be accomplished.

INCOMPARABLE VIRTUES

AUSTERITY CANNOT COMPARE TO IMPERTUBAbility. No happiness on earth can compare to the bliss of contentment.

THERE IS NO VIRTUE COMPARABLE TO compassion.

ALWAYS REMEMBER THAT GREED IS THE MOST fatal vice.

ONE MUST CAST ASIDE ONE'S GREED, AND SEEK to possess the virtues of impertubability, contentment and compassion, if one wishes to achieve something in this life.

REACH FOR FELICITY

ANGER IS LIKE YAMARAJ, LORD OF DEATH ANGER is synonymous with destruction, and it will ultimately lead to death.

DESIRE IS LIKE THE VAITARNI, (RIVER OF HELL) for it courses recklessly through the human heart, and ultimately flings man into the infernal fire. Because of desire, man is forced to face all kinds of suffering.

KNOWLEDGE CAN BE COMPARED TO Kamadhenu, (in Indian mythology, Kamadhenu, the sacred cow, belongs to Indra. Kamadhenu yielded Indra all that he desired.) for it will provide you with all that you require, at an oppurtune moment.

CONTENTMENT IS LIKE NANDANVAN (ELYSIUM, the garden of Indra), as it gives one endless felicity.

THE USE AND SIGNIFICANCE OF VIRTUE

BEAUTY HAS NO SIGNIFICANCE UNLESS IT IS accompanied by virtue. The magnificence of an ancestry, lies in the modesty and amiability of its members. The splendour of education lies in original thought, accomplishment and perfection. The value of money lies in its use.

EVEN AN ABSOLUTELY BEWITCHING WOMAN, will look quite contemptible, if she is devoid of virtue. Though a person may hail from a renowned ancestry, if he is devoid of modesty and congeniality, then he will be a despicable specimen. A superior education will be of no avail, if it fails to make one an accomplished person. And finally, money will lose all its meaning if it is locked away in an iron safe. Money is useless in the hands of a miser.

CONFORMANCE

A DISCONTENTED BRAHMIN, A CONTENT KING,

a bashful prostitute and a brazen wife, can never find happiness.

IT IS THE VIRTUE OF CONTENTMENT THAT makes a man a Brahmin in the true sense of the word. If a Brahmin shows discontentment, then he is no longer worthy of being a Brahmin. Discontentment will always be a black mark against him.

A CONTENT MAN SHOULD NEVER BE CROWNED king. If a king is content, he will never be able to expand his kingdom. A king should be ambitious, and should never miss an opportunity to expand his kingdom. Contentment will be an enormous drawback for a king.

PROSTITUTION REQUIRES A CERTAIN DEGREE of boldness. Therefore a coy prostitute can never succeed in captivating her customers.

IT MUST ALSO BE NOTED, THAT IF A WIFE behaves like a wanton hussy, then her husband may eventually abandon her.

VIRTUE AND VICE ARE PURELY RELATIVE. THEY can be determined, only by keeping the time, place, and circumstance in view. What is a merit for one is often a flaw for the other. One must always conform to one's position in life.

SIGNIFICANCE OF KNOWLEDGE

A SCHOLAR IS UNIVERSALLY ADORED. HE IS admired by people, irrespective of whether he is in his own country or not. Knowledge is a powerful asset in his hands, and it confers universal adulation upon him. A knowledgable and erudite man can achieve anything.

THE ILLITERATE MAN MAY BELONG TO AN illustrious family, he may be wealthy and attractive, yet the truth remains that only erudition can gain him widespread esteem. An ignorant man is like a flower without fragrance. He is a burden on the world – a mere animal in the form of a man.

IT IS KNOWLEDGE, THAT GIVES ONE RESPECTAbility – not one's fascinating persona, affluence or lineage.

INVALUABLE ADVICE

A MAN WHO OPENS HIS HEART TO OTHERS, will meet a tragic end. If one is concerned about one's welfare, then one should take care never to reveal one's heart. It would be wise to act upon such invaluable advice. He, who pays little heed to such counsel, will die as miserably as a snake trapped in its hole. One who acts upon such guidance, will remain invulnerable and invincible.

SLEEP

IF ONE SHOULD SEE EITHER A STUDENT, servant, traveller, storekeeper, door-keeper or a starved man, deep in sleep, then one should wake them up at once. A student who falls asleep will not be able to pursue his studies. A servant who is asleep cannot serve his master. A traveller who falls asleep will not be able to reach his destination. A famished man who falls asleep, will awake only to feel the pangs of hunger. The storekeeper in deep sleep, is unable to serve food, and the door-keeper who is deep in slumber, is unable to protect us from thieves and intruders.

ON THE CONTRARY, IF ONE SHOULD SEE A snake, lion, wasp, child, dog, imbecile or king, deep in sleep, one should refrain from awaking them. A snake may bite; a lion may devour one; a wasp may sting; a child may weep; a dog may bite or bark; an imbecile may abuse one; and a king may get annoyed.

LIMITS OF DECENCY

A BRAHMIN WHO EXPOUNDS THE VEDAS, OUT of an insatiable greed for money, and eats food from the hands of fallen men, is like a poisonous snake. He is not a true Brahmin.

IT IS DETESTABLE TO TRANSGRESS THE LIMITS of decency. When a man goes beyond these limits, he is robbed of his dignity, integrity and might. He will look utterly undignified.

OSTENTATION

EVEN IF A SNAKE IS NOT POISONOUS, IT should not stop hissing under any circumstance. The snake will have only its hiss to ward off human beings and protect itself. Without this protective pretence, even a little child could stone it to death.

A LITTLE OSTENTATION IS NECESSARY IN THIS world without the minimum of ostentation, a man's worth will remain unrecognised.

ON IDLE GOSSIP

ONE SHOULD NOT WASTE ONE'S TIME, AND dissipate one's energy, gossiping with gamblers, bandits and women. If one wishes to reach the pinnacle of earthly success, it is absolutely necessary to observe taciturnity. Curbing loose talk is a sure key to success.

THE IMPOVERISHED SOUL

A POVERTY-STRICKEN MAN SHOULD NOT BE regarded as an impoverished soul. He could achieve worldly prosperity at any time in his future. When Fate smiles upon him, he is sure to earn abundantly.

AN ILLITERATE MAN WILL ALWAYS REMAIN poor and deprived. When a man is illiterate and ignorant, the world will seem distasteful and barren to him.

INDIVIDUAL NATURES

IS THERE ANY LIMIT TO A POET'S IMAGINATION? Is there anything that a woman is incapable of? Is there any obscenity that a drunkard will not use? Is there anything that a crow finds inedible? Man can only live according to his nature, and all his deeds will be a manifestation of his essential disposition.

ANTAGONISM

THE BEGGAR'S GREATEST ENEMY IS THE MISER. A beggar can tolerate the presence of a wealthy man, but he would be unable to endure the company of a miser, even for a while. Whosoever should hinder the fulfilment of one's desires, is perceived as one's enemy.

An idiot will always regard his advisor as his enemy. An adulterous woman will always look upon her husband as her foe. The moon will always be the greatest enemy of thieves on the prowl.

BESTIAL MAN

WHO CAN BE DEFINED AS AN ANIMAL?

A MAN WHO IS NEITHER LEARNED NOR accomplished, who does not possess a charitable and humble nature, and who does not adhere to principles of duty and obligation, is nothing but a burden on this world. One who has such blemishes in his character, can be defined as a animal.

A CRY IN THE WILDERNESS

IT WOULD BE FOOLISH OF AN INSTRUCTOR TO advise one who lacked depth and seriousness. Such shallow men are like the snakes who have their abode on Malachal Hills. These snakes are impervious to the heady fragrance of sandalwood in the Malachal hills. Even the hills on which the sandalwood grows, remain uninfluenced by its fragrance. One must understand that, there is little point in advising those who are not earnest and receptive. The exercise is as futile as crying in the wilderness. Good advice is always wasted on frivolous souls, who refuse to take life seriously.

THE VIRUE OF RECEPTIVITY

IF A MAN IS NOT SOLEMN AND RECEPTIVE, could he possibly imbibe the essence of the Scriptures? Can he who is blind see his reflection in the mirror? The Scriptures can be grasped only by those, who are solemn, humble and receptive. If a man is devoid of these virtues, he will never be able to assimilate the essence of the Scriptures. He will merely be able to cram them, as a parrot would.

INCORRIGIBILITY

AN INCORRIGIBLE MAN CANNOT BE converted into a saint, unless he has a powerful yearning to become one. How can you redeem one who is irredeemable? However thoroughly an anus is cleansed, it will always remain an unsanctified anus.

HOSTILITY

IT IS NOT ADVISABLE TO HARBOUR FEELINGS of animosity towards those who are more eminent and powerful. Under no circumstances, should one antagonise a Brahmin.

IF ONE RAISES A BRAHMIN'S WRATH, HE WILL curse one's entire clan.

IT IS NOT ADVISABLE TO BE HOSTILE EVEN TO one's juniors. One may gain the upper hand, but such a conflict will mar one's dignity and reputation.

CHARITY

TO LIVE AS A PAUPER, AT THE MERCY OF ONE'S kith and kin, is the singularly most unpleasant experience, that any individual could have. It is far better to live in seclusion in a dense forest, in the company of tigers, lions, snakes and other wild animals. Living an isolated and austere life, is far more gratifying than a life of penury at the mercy of relatives. It is far better to eat off a plate of leaves, than eat off a plate of gold, that was given to one as charity.

A BRAHMINS REALITY

A BRAHMIN'S EXISTENCE IS COMPARABLE TO that of a tree. A Brahmins root is 'sandhya' (it is compulsory for a Brahmin to offer these prayers at dawn and twilight). 'sharda' (Saraswati, Goddess of knowledge and music) evokes his compassion. But his crowning leaves are his exemplary deeds. A Brahmin must always protect his root, and offer Sandhya; for once the root is destroyed, he will have no compassion or laudable deeds to speak off. The tree of his life will be barren.

TRANSIENCE OF LIFE

AS NIGHT FALLS, BIRDS TAKE SHELTER IN THE trees. And when dawn breaks, they soar into the wide blue yonder. Similarly, our life on this earth, must be perceived as an overnight stay. We all meet on this planet, and foster ties with a variety of people. But ultimately, we are all yanked apart by a powerful Fate, and carried towards our final destination.

PRUDENCE VERSUS STRENGTH

MIGHT IS USELESS, UNLESS IT IS BACKED BY prudence.

IF ONE BEHAVES WITHOUT CAUTION, EVEN A weaker enemy can vanquish one.

CAN ONE FORGET THE FABLE OF THE PRUDENT rabbit, who destroyed the powerful lion by showing him his own reflection in the well? One must always employ the most lethal weapons, but if one is not backed by caution, even the most destructive weapons will be rendered useless. An unarmed man, blessed with the power of sagacity, can easily defeat a man, equipped with mighty weapons.

LIMITATION

A MAN WHO CONSTANTLY CROSSES HIS LIMITS, is not deceived by others; he deceives himself. If a King, conveniently ignores the restraints that his title imposes upon him, and lives a prurient life, then he is inviting his own denigration, not to mention endless suffering. One should be careful never to cross one's limits.

POWER

A GIGANTIC ELEPHANT CAN BE CONTROLLED by a mere iron hook (ankush).

A SMALL LAMP CAN LIGHT UP A VAST STRETCH of darkness.

INDRA'S THUNDERBOLT CAN MAKE THE largest mountains crumble.

HOW CAN THE STRENGTH OF AN IRON HOOK compare to that of an enormous elephant? How can one compare the luminescence of the small lamp to the all-engulfing darkness? How could the bolt of lightning destroy the mighty mountain?

WHO IS TRULY POWERFUL? THINK OVER IT.

AN INDISPUTABLE TRUTH

CAN A MAN WHO IS A MEAT-EATER EVER BE compassionate? Can one who behaves in a lecherous manner, ever become pure of heart? Will one ever find meat in a vulture's nest? It is impossible! Similiarly, it is impossible for a man to succeed in completing his education, if he is wrapped up in household affairs; He can never become an accomplished man.

CONDITIONING

WICKEDNESS IS INGRAINED IN CERTAIN MEN. Such men can never give up their villainous ways.

EVEN IF ONE FEEDS MILK TO A SNAKE, IT WILL continue to spew venom. Similiarly, no amount of sugarcane juice poured at the root of the margosa tree, can sweeten its essence. The margosa tree is quintessentially bitter. Nothing can remove its pungent sourness.

CHURLISH REACTION

WHEN ONE IS UNABLE TO OBTAIN A, particular thing, or when one is unaware of its worth, then one is always quick to denounce it.

MAN IS SIMILIAR TO THE FOX IN THE FAMED fable. Even after much frisking and frolicking, the fox was unable to reach the grapes on the vine. In a fit of despondency, the fox cried, "Oh, the grapes are so sour!". And he walked away.

MERITORIOUSNESS

MERITORIOUS PEOPLE NEVER HAVE possessive natures. This is why their fame knows no bounds. Lord Krishna and King Vikramaditya were known for their magnanimity. Whatever they possessed, they shared generously with others. Their magnanimity of spirit earned them great recognition.

OBSERVE THE HONEY BEES! THEY ARE FULLY aware that the honey they have painstakingly accumulated will be plundered by others. Regardless of this, they silently proceed with their strenuous task. It is this altruistic attitude, that fetches them great renown.

ONE MUST PERFORM LAUDABLE DEEDS TO attain worldly eminence. A man cannot earn fame without noble conduct. Fame and eminence will only emerge from meritorious conduct.

SHUDRA

THOSE WHO SELL OIL, FLOWERS, HONEY, GHEE, wine or meat for their livelihood, are known as Shudras.

THE ROGUE

A HYPOCRITE, WHO IS ENVIOUS OF OTHERS, impedes the fulfilment of another's desires, desecrates the pond, the garden, or the temple, robs his master of his wealth, and enters into illicit relationships, to fulfil his selfish desires, can be labelled a perfect rogue.

A MAN'S ACTIONS WILL ALWAYS REVEAL THE true nature of his being.

IT IS SAID THAT A CAT AND A ROGUE HAVE similar temperaments.

INFLUENCE

THE COMPANY OF SAINTLY PERSONS WILL, NO doubt, transform one into a virtuous soul. But one who is truly saintly can never be influenced by another's wicked ways. Though a flower can never possess the rich smell of the earth, the fragrance of the flower is buried deep within the earth. A truly virtuous man will always remain pure. Even the most adverse circumstances will not be able to destroy his innate purity.

THOUGH A SAINTLY PERSON HAS THE POWER to cleanse the mind of a wicked man, his own virtue will always remain unblemished.

UNIQUENESS OF PERCEPTION

JUST AS EACH INDIVIDUAL IS UNIQUE, EQUALLY unique is his perception of joy. A Brahmin is delighted when invited for a meal. A cultured woman derives satisfaction from her husband's happiness. The Minister rejoices when his King admires his capable ways. A licentious man is satisfied when he has assuaged his lust with intercourse. A wicked man delights in persecuting others. A prostitute's joy knows no bounds, when she sees her customer at her doorstep.

STRANGE AND UNIQUE ARE THE INDIVIDUAL perceptions of happiness.

A TRUE BRAHMIN

ONE, WHO TREATS ALL WOMEN AS HE WOULD his own mother; who does not feel envious at the earthly prosperity of another; and who treats beggar and king alike, is a true Brahmin.

LEARNING

ONE SHOULD LEARN AFFABILITY FROM THE sons of the King. To acquire nobility and virtue, one must approach sages. In order to become proficient in the art of deceit, one must strike up a friendship with a gambler.

STRANGELY, AT TIMES, THE IGNORANCE OF THE ignorant is more instructive than the wisdom of the wise.

FOOD

A WISE MAN IS NEVER OBSESSED WITH FOOD. He accepts that food is essential if one is to survive, but he does not live for food. Why do men lend such significance to food? Even a street dog can find a way to fill his stomach, with something or the other.

AGE

WILL ONE'S VIRTUES DIMINISH AS ONE GETS older? Of course not. When a pomegranate ripens, it becomes sweeter than before. Similiarly as men age, they attain a greater level of maturity and wisdom.

ABSTINENCE

SAINTS ARE MEN OF DIVINE CONDUCT. SUCH men are immune to the lure of money. Though they may receive money in plenty, their detachment from worldly life enables them to cast it aside and walk on.

EVEN A FASCINATING WOMAN WOULD FIND IT virtually impossible to seduce an upright man, using her bewitching looks and coquettish ways. A man of honour can exercise complete restraint over his senses.

A MAN WHO HAS RENOUNCED THE WORLD IS firm in his resolve to attain enlightenment. He resolutely adheres to the principles of honour and virtue, regardless of the innumerable impediments that he may come accross.

IT IS THE VIRTUOUS MAN'S OBSERVANCE OF abstinence that makes such incredible self-restraint possible. Only a self-disciplined man, with a will of iron, can finally conquer this world.

THE SUBJECT WILL BE AS THE KING IS

IF A KING IS RIGHTEOUS, HIS SUBJECTS WILL doubtless follow his noble path. But if the king is a morally depraved soul, his subjects are most likely to follow in his footsteps, and live licentious lives. Hence the adage "the subjects will be as the king is." This is an eternal truth.

RIGHTEOUSNESS

FEW WICKED MEN ARE REMEMBERED AFTER their death. But the righteous man, who has lived an exemplary life, will live on in people's hearts, even after his demise. His memory inspires the living to tread the path of integrity. History is evidence to this fact.

WORTHLESSNESS

HOW CAN A COW'S UDDERS BE OF ANY BENEFIT to her, if she cannot produce any milk? Similiarly, if a man has neither integrity nor affluence; if he has neither a sense of duty nor a desire to free himself from worldly bondage, then he is of no use to this world.

ENVY

FAILURE IS THE ROOT CAUSE OF ENVY. WHEN an unsuccessful man bears witness to the worldly accomplishments of another, his heart burns with envy. A man who is consumed by the flames of envy, suffers a loss of dignity and self-respect. He falls in his own eyes.

AUTHENTIC JEWELS

A FOOLISH MAN GIVES INORDINATE importance to the jewels he has in his possession. But they are merely worthless stones. Little does he know that the real gems are food, water and mellifluent speech. Man can live without precious jewels, but can he survive without food and water? Never!

THE HUMAN BODY

IF ONE'S WIFE HAS ELOPED, THERE IS A possibility that she could return. And one can always retrieve lost wealth and lost land. But one possesses one's body only once. Use it well.

UNITY

UNITY IS AN AMAZINGLY POWERFUL CONCEPT. Thousands of scattered straws can easily be crushed by an elephant. But, when these straws are tightly bound together, they can thrash a gigantic elephant, and bring him under control.

DISCLOSURE

IF ONE REVEALS ONE'S SECRETS TO A WICKED man, they will soon become the talk of the town. A short conversation with a magnanimous man, will most likely develop into a lengthy dialogue on charitability. A learned man will open his heart to a sincere and eligible disciple, and he will bequeath him the wealth of his scriptural knowledge.

REMEMBER – A DROP OF OIL, SPILT ON THE water, quickly spreads over it's surface.

ASTONISHMENT

WHY IS ONE CONSTANTLY AMAZED AT THE presence of virtue in others? There are many who are charitable, affable, valourous, tactful and learned. There is no dearth of men of exemplary nature. But one should not lose the sight of the fact, that there is no man, whose virtue cannot be surpassed.

BONDING OF THE SPIRIT

LOVE SHORTENS ALL DISTANCES AND BRIDGES all gaps. If your companion does not have a place in your heart, then physical proximity is meaningless. He will be a million miles away from you in spirit.

BEWARE OF THE KNAVE

A KNAVE MAY UTTER "RAM RAM", AND STILL hide a knife behind his back. When a favourable opportunity arises, he will withdraw his marvellous knife to stab one in the back. Just as the hunter traps the poor deer with his melodious song, the knave will use mellifluent speech to realise his selfish motives. He is a wolf in sheep's clothing. The adage "Those who are too courteous are bound to be far too crafty" is applicable to such a man.

HANDLING THE KNAVE

ONLY CORRUPT MEANS CAN BE USED TO handle a knave. Only diamonds can cut diamonds. A thorn must be used to remove a thorn. Remember this eternal truth.

CIRCUMSPECTION

ONE SHOULD ALWAYS THINK TWICE BEFORE developing a close relationship with a woman, a preceptor and a king. Ideally, they should be kept at arms length, as a difference of opinion could arise at any time.

A WISE MAN

A WISE MAN IS ONE WHOSE SPEECH IS ALWAYS perfectly suited to the situation. He fosters ties with those who have similiar temperaments, and displays his anger in a manner befitting his superior status. He is proficient in the Scriptures and devoid of any vice.

DETERMINANT OF ACTIONS

IT IS TRUE THAT EACH HUMAN BEING'S perception is unique. Whereas the enlightened man perceives the body as something perishable, a debauched individual sees it as an object to gratify his strong sexual desires.

A MAN'S NATURE DETERMINES HIS PERCEPtion, and his perception determines his actions.

THRIFT

WHEN A MAN IS POOR AND DESTITUTE, THEN his family and friends are quick to desert him. But when he attains affluence, the very same people will mill around him. A man is judged not by his qualities, but by his wealth. Therefore, one should be close-fisted, and avoid all extravagance.

APT TREATMENT

ONE'S MANAGEMENT OF A SITUATION IS A factor of paramount importance in determining success in life. A man of substance can transform even the trivial into the sublime. But a notorious man attempting a good deed is sure to become the object of ridicule.

ELIXIR GIVES LIFE, BUT IF IT IS ADMINISTERED by an incompetent man, it can bring about one's death. Yet, miraculously, even though Lord Shiva consumed poison, he gained more power and veneration.

UNCONDITIONAL LOVE AND HUMILITY

A REAL FRIENDSHIP IS BASED ON UNCONDITIONAL love and affection. If the moment demands a sacrifice, then a true friend would not hesitate to give up his life. A man who is pure of heart is the very embodiment of wisdom and righteousness. He can never be accused of arrogance and false vanity.

IRREPRESSIBLE TRUTH

VARIOUS JEWELS MAY LOOK CHEAPER THAN plain glass, but their real worth cannot be concealed forever. One day the truth must surface.

EVEN THOUGH PAPER FLOWERS MAY BE prettier than the real ones, they can never issue an authentic balmy fragrance.

THE HEINOUS CRIMINAL

WHO IS BRANDED A HEINOUS CRIMINAL?

HE, WHO DOES NOT PROVIDE SHELTER OR respite to one who has come from a distant land; who does not serve his guest before serving himself; and who furtively usurps other's wealth and property, is a heinous criminal and the very incarnation of Sin.

HELL

WHO GOES TO HELL?

HE WHO LIVES AN OSTENTATIOUS LIFE, AND IS constantly given to spouting profanity, is most likely to go to hell.

GLORY OF SELF-RELIANCE

A MAN WHO IS DEPENDENT ON ANOTHER WILL always look petty and insignificant before him.

THE MOON DEPENDS ON THE SUN TO illuminate it. Therefore, when the sun shines brightly in the sky, the moon is obscured by its dazzling splendour.

SIMILIARLY, A MAN WHO TAKES REFUGE IN another's house will always be treated as a lesser being. He will be forced to suffer great humiliation and neglect. It is therefore, necessary to be self-reliant. One must stand on one's own feet.

CONTENTMENT WITH ONE'S LOT

AS LONG AS THE BHOINRA STAYS WITHIN THE petals of the lotus, it will contentedly savour its juice and balmy fragrance. When it cannot find the lotus, it turns to the flower of Torya (a kind of vegetable also called lentil), and that is more than enough. It is better to have morsels of food then to die of starvation. Something is always better than nothing. One should make the most of one's portion in life.

THE APPROPRIATE MOMENT

THE NIGHTINGALE ONLY SINGS DURING THE rains. Only if the time and place are appropriate, does this bird burst into melodious song. Birds and animals always behave with respect to the season. The suitability of time and place is of paramount importance to them. Men, who do not speak at appropriate moments are far worse than the birds and the animals. A poet and a singer are respected only if they gauge the standard of their audience before performing. A poet will become an object of ridicule, if he recites his poem before people who are incapable of appreciating it.

INSTRINSIC SIMILIARITY

IS THERE ANYONE ON EARTH, WHO HAS NOT displayed arrogance, after acquiring earthly wealth? Is there anyone who is not intoxicated by prosperity?

IS THERE ANYONE, WHO REMAINS unbewitched, after catching a glimpse of an enchanting woman?

IS THERE ANY MAN WHOSE MOUTH DOES NOT water at the sight of delicious food?

DEATH IS AN OMNIPRESENT FORCE. IS THERE anyone who has conquered it?

IS THERE ANYONE WHO HAS NEVER BEHAVED in a vile manner?

WE ARE ALL MERE MORTALS. OUR FOLLIES ARE human. Human nature is such that all men are intrinsically similiar. Most differences observed are superficial.

MISFORTUNE

IT IS SAID THAT WHEN MISFORTUNE APPEARS, intuitive intelligence deserts one.

NO ONE CAN CLAIM TO HAVE SEEN A GOLDEN deer. Yet, prior to her preordained abduction, Sita swore she had seen one. At her behest, Rama frantically chased the golden deer to capture it. He only wished to fulfil his beloved wife's desire. It is in his absence that Sita was abducted by Ravana.

MISFORTUNE IS OFTEN PREORDAINED. ONE inevitably abandons rational thinking at such a time.

PRETENTIOUSNESS

IT IS ONLY THE WEAK MAN WHO PRETENDS TO be a saint. Truly powerful men are rarely inclined towards a saintly life.

IT IS VERY DIFFICULT FOR A BEAUTIFUL YOUNG woman, with a captivating figure, to be totally faithful to her husband. Yet, an old woman who has neglected her body, will pretentiously adhere to the marriage vows, and remain devoted to her husband.

PRETENTIOUSNESS AND HYPOCRISY ARE deeply entrenched in the human psyche.

SANCTITY OF THE HEART

IF GOD RESIDES IN A MAN'S HEART, THEN HE has nothing to gain from rigorous and austere exercises. What further benefit can he derive from visiting sacred pilgrim centres? When a man is the very embodiment of honesty and integrity, his dwelling assumes the sanctity of a pilgrim centre.

SHINING VIRTUE

VIRTUE IS CHERISHED THE WORLD OVER. A wealthy man can never be as revered as a virtuous man.

VIRTUE ALWAYS SPEAKS FOR ITSELF. PEOPLE will always look down upon a man who prattles about his own virtue. If one is truly virtuous, intuitive men will acknowledge one's worth. One cannot expect cobblers to recognise the true worth of a jewel; only jewellers can do that.

WHEN A WISE MAN POSSESSES VIRTUE, THE quality has a lustre that is impossible to ignore.

INSATIABLE GREED

MAN'S THIRST FOR LIFE, SEX, MONEY AND food are insatiable. As far as these things are concerned, he is never content with what he has. There is always a frantic greed for more. Sadly the more he gets, the more intense his discontentment is.

THE LIGHTEST ENTITY

STRAW HAS NO WEIGHT TO SPEAK OF.

COTTON IS EVEN LIGHTER THEN STRAW.

BUT THE LIGHTEST ENTITY IS UNDOUBTEDLY the beggar.

YET EVEN THE BREEZE WILL NOT CARRY HIM away, lest he should ask something of it.

A LIFE OF DISGRACE

IT IS BETTER TO DIE, THAN TO HUMILIATE oneself living a life tainted by disgrace. One experiences the pain of death only for a split second. But it is agonising to suffer disrespect throughout one's life.

NOBLE AND SACRED DEEDS

THE NOBLEST ACT IS THAT OF GIVING AWAY food in charity.

DWADASHI (THE TWELFTH DAY OF EACH HALF of the lunar month), is the day that possesses the greatest sanctity.

OF ALL THE SHLOKAS, GAYATRI MANTRA (recited daily by a true Brahmin) is the most sacred shloka.

FINALLY, NO DEITY ON EARTH, MUST BE MORE revered than one's own mother.

THE STRENGTH OF A VIRTUE

THOUGH THE KETKI HAS THORNS IN abundance, its powerful fragrance gains it universal admiration. Even if a man has only a single virtue, if it is nurtured properly, and used to advantage, then it will most certainly overshadow all his vices.

ILLICIT KNOWLEDGE

SHOULD A MAN, WHO HAS NOT BEEN initiated by a master, acquire scriptural knowledge, he will be as stigmatised as a woman, who is impregnated during the course of an adulterous relationship. It is imperative for one to be initiated by a master, before one ventures upon the path of Truth.

INAUSPICIOUS ACTS

GAZING AT ONE'S OWN REFLECTION IN THE water, shaving off one's hair at a barber's dwelling, and using sandal that has been rubbed on stone, are all considered to be inauspicious acts.

GOING TO ANOTHER'S HOUSE AS AN uninvited guest, interrupting a conversation between two people, and indiscriminately giving away one's belongings, are considered to be signs of stupidity.

INTELLECTUAL CHOICE

EXCESSIVE CONSUMPTION OF KUNDRU (a creeper whose fruits are used as a vegetable), can blunt one's intellect; but when consumed discriminately, it can only sharpen it. The Almighty God often imbues the same thing with diametrically opposite qualities. How one uses particular things at particular times vastly depends on the intellect's discriminatory ability. Everything is available on earth. One can reach out to both vice and virtue. What one accepts or rejects, depends on one's intellect. The choice will reflect one's inner quality.

PLAY OF DESTINY

THE CONCH SHELL COMES FROM THE DEPTHS of the ocean – a treasure trove of jewels. Laxmi (Goddess of wealth), lavishes material affection upon it.

BUT WHEN THE CONCH FALLS INTO THE hands of a beggar, it serves as a tool for begging. The blameless conch is helpless before this twist of fate. Oh friends! powerful and strange is the play of destiny.

THE PATH TO SELF-REALISATION

WEARING PRETTY BANGLES WILL NOT beautify one's hands; doing charitable deeds will. Smearing sandal paste over one's body will not cleanse it as a bath will. Emancipation from worldly life can only be achieved through knowledge. One who lives a pretentious life, can never attain enlightenment. Contentment can be realised only by those who live a dignified life. As long as one fails to grasp this truth, one will drift aimlessly on the sea of worldly existence.

LATITUDINARISM

BOTH A WOMAN WHO SNORES IN HER SLEEP, and a man who disrobes himself before going to sleep, lessen their life span. Copulating in the day-time, and gambling into the wee hours, will also shorten the duration of one's life. Life on earth is governed by certain rules and regulations. Violating these rules can bring one needless suffering. It never pays to be a latitudinarian!

FUTILITY OF OUTER APPEARANCE

HOW CAN AN ANT EVER COMPARE TO AN elephant? Yet inspite of the disparity in their sizes, both co-exist peacefully on this planet.

IT IS IMPORTANT NOT BE TAKEN IN BY THE forms and figures of living beings. Instead, one must learn to appreciate their actions, merits and virtues. Lord Shiva wore matted hair; Ganesha had an elephant trunk; and Ashtavakra had a deformed body. Yet, to this day, they are highly revered all over the world.

THE OUTER APPEARANCE IS NOTHING BUT A mere superficial detail. What is significant is wisdom, strength and inner beauty.

ERUDITION

EVEN THOUGH THE COW EATS A VARIETY OF things, it continues to provide us with milk. Is there anything that cannot be made out of milk? It gives us curd, whey, butter, ghee and cheese.

SIMILIARLY, WHATEVER THE LEARNED MAN does, he does with a purpose. His actions are truly worthy of imitation. Only a wise man can comprehend the utility and worth of the actions of other wise men.

SLAVES OF HABIT

A SNAKE'S BODY WILL WIND AND CURVE AS IT slithers along; a dog's tail will always be twisted; a donkey will always take pride in displaying the strength of his legs; and flies and black ants will always return to familiar surroundings.

IN A SIMILIAR WAY, MAN IS ALSO A SLAVE TO HIS habits. Human beings are totally enslaved by their habits and addictions.

HYPOCRISY

THE TEETH THAT THE ELEPHANT USES TO chew his food are always obscured from view.

THERE ARE FEW PEOPLE ON EARTH, WHO ARE not hypocrites. Man is a two-faced creature. He does not hesitate to reveal his respectable front to the world. The darker aspects of his personality always remain hidden from public view.

INTRINSIC WORTH

LORD KRISHNA JOINED THE COWHERDESSES in a passionate and erotic dance. As his period of banishment came to a close, Arjuna was forced to become a eunuch. Shantanu, unfortunately, developed a fascination for a fisherman's daughter.

YES, ALL GREAT MEN HAVE BEEN PREY TO certain moral frailties and character defects. But must one follow that pattern, and constantly highlight the shortcomings of such revered men? One must realise their instrinsic worth, and dismiss as insignificant, their doings during their earthly sojourn.

EXCRUCIATING COMPANY

A WISE MAN ALWAYS BYPASSES A MAD MAN, a beautiful young woman, a leper, and a rogue masquerading as a Sadhu. It is distressing to be in their company. One should always salute them from afar, and walk away.

AUSPICIOUSNESS

COMING ACROSS A SINNER ON TEMPLE premises; a corpse being carried on the bier by four men; or a child on a mother's lap, is considered auspicious. Seeing them from afar is an enlightening experience, for they reflect both the mystery and the reality of our world. They are conducive to our spiritual transformation.

EFFORT

LUCK ALWAYS INVOLVES A MINIMUM OF diligence. One cannot lie idle beneath a mango tree, and expect a ripe mango to fall into one's hands. Luck will always elude one, who is unwilling to take pains to achieve his aims.

COMPATABILITY

JUST AS OIL AND GHEE WILL NEVER MIX WITH water, it is not possible for two individuals with diametrically opposite natures, to rub shoulders with each other.

THE FORCE OF TIME

TIME IS AN UNSTOPPABLE FORCE. IT MOVES ON relentlessly. A man who understands the value of time is assured of success in life. Always avoid procrastination! Remain vigilant, and honour time.

WINE AND WOMEN

WOMEN ALLURE ONE WITH FALSE SHOWS OF love. Wine entraps one with promises of pleasure. Oh imbecile, do you know the consequences of giving into such pleasure? You will die the death of a worm. Wine and women will creep into your life to rob you of you wealth and talent. Beware of them – or you will have to atone for your sinful ways.

JAICO PUBLISHING HOUSE

Elevate Your Life. Transform Your World.

ESTABLISHED IN 1946, Jaico Publishing House is home to world-transforming authors such as Sri Sri Paramahansa Yogananda, Osho, The Dalai Lama, Sri Sri Ravi Shankar, Robin Sharma, Deepak Chopra, Jack Canfield, Eknath Easwaran, Devdutt Pattanaik, Khushwant Singh, John Maxwell, Brian Tracy and Stephen Hawking.

Our late founder Mr. Jaman Shah first established Jaico as a book distribution company. Sensing that independence was around the corner, he aptly named his company Jaico ('Jai' means victory in Hindi). In order to service the significant demand for affordable books in a developing nation, Mr. Shah initiated Jaico's own publications. Jaico was India's first publisher of paperback books in the English language.

While self-help, religion and philosophy, mind/body/spirit, and business titles form the cornerstone of our non-fiction list, we publish an exciting range of travel, current affairs, biography, and popular science books as well. Our renewed focus on popular fiction is evident in our new titles by a host of fresh young talent from India and abroad. Jaico's recently established Translations Division translates selected English content into nine regional languages.

Jaico's Higher Education Division (HED) is recognized for its student-friendly textbooks in Business Management and Engineering which are in use countrywide.

In addition to being a publisher and distributor of its own titles, Jaico is a major national distributor of books of leading international and Indian publishers. With its headquarters in Mumbai, Jaico has branches and sales offices in Ahmedabad, Bangalore, Bhopal, Bhubaneswar, Chennai, Delhi, Hyderabad, Kolkata and Lucknow.

SINCE 1946